THE CROW ★ STEVE MARTIN

NEW SONGS FOR THE FIVE-STRING BANJO BY STEVE MARTIN & TRANSCRIBED BY TONY TRISCHKA

All Songs Written by Steve Martin
(unless otherwise noted)
Songs Copyright © 2009 by Steve Martin

Art Directors: G. Carr & Salli Ratts
Music Inscription: Andrew DuBrock
Steve Martin photo by Sandee O. Photography

ISBN # 978-1-59773-277-2

© 2009 Homespun Tapes, Ltd.
Box 340, Woodstock, NY 12498
www.homespun.com

BUY THESE FUN BOOKS

TABLE OF CONTENTS

INTRODUCTION

Steve Martin is a banjo genius!

And his brand new (as of this writing) CD, *The Crow*, proves it. (Steve preferred I not gush on like this, but I'll explain).

Steve won't knock your socks in the creek with blazing pyrotechnics as he spider-walks every inch of the neck from open position to the twenty second fret in three seconds flat. But he does get around that fingerboard, thank you very much. And I suppose he's not as influential as Earl Scruggs. But in his own quiet way, he has expanded the capabilities and range of the banjo. This may have something to do with the fact that he's been primarily self-taught since high school. He just thinks differently. Oh yeah, and he also wrote fourteen out of the fifteen tunes you'll find in this tab tome. They're beautiful, interesting and varied.

Like Earl, most of what Steve does falls very comfortably under the fingers. But it sounds and feels fresh. For one thing, Steve is not a slave to G tuning. There are a bunch of tunes in D tuning, G with a raised second string, double C, G with the fifth string up to A. You get the idea. So you're going down the path less traveled, with the signs pointing in different directions.

Steve's rolls roll out differently too. Sure, there are forward and backward rolls, etc., but he mixes in what I call the "Steve Roll." This is unofficial terminology, and refers to a right-hand move that crops up in many of his tunes. It's easy and refers to a first string-fifth string-first string move. Initially, I noticed it in "The Crow", but it does appear in "Words Unspoken" and others as well. I've stolen it a number of times when I hit a roll wall while working up a fiddle tune. Works like a charm…..kind of a banjoistic "Get Out of Jail Free" card.

Steve's also as adept at clawhammer as he is at fingerpicking. Not too many folks can make that claim. He also composes fluently in both. If you only pick, this is the opportunity you've been waiting for to burnish your fledgling clawhammer chops.

Now, for some background:

Steve and my band Breakfast Special shared the bill at a small Greenwich Village club back in 1974. Steve's whole career lay before him, and this was just a footnote along the way to bigger and more remunerative things. He had the arrow through the head, he was quite hilarious, and, of all things, he was playing some really nice banjo.

In the mid '80s Steve recorded an album called *The Steve Martin Brothers*. One side was comedy, the other, original banjo music. Amongst the sidemen were Vassar Clements and Junior Huskey. It was wonderfully different…mostly finger-picking but not necessarily Scruggsy. His film career continued apace. His banjo career had not yet stormed the parapets.

Fast forward to 2001. Earl Scruggs released an album called *Earl Scruggs and Friends*. In addition to such bluegrass redoubtables as Elton John and Sting, Earl asked Steve to pick along on "Foggy Mountain Breakdown." The album won a Grammy and Steve decided to get more serious about his already fine banjo playing.

In 2005 Steve assembled Men With Banjos (Who Know How to Use Them) for an appearance at The New Yorker Festival. A spot on David Letterman helped promote the festival, with Steve, Earl Scruggs, Pete Wernick, Tony Ellis and Charles Wood powering their way through "Foggy Mountain Breakdown." You couldn't ask for a better banjo booster than Steve.

A few years later I asked Steve to join me on my CD *Double Banjo Bluegrass Spectacular.* He graciously acceded to my request. We ended up recording *The Crow*, and had the pleasure of performing it on the Ellen, Letterman, and Regis shows. Even though we were ostensibly promoting *my* new album, with many fine original songs, *his* became the breakout banjo hit, with all the trappings that entails.

After that spate of activity, Steve sat in with my band for a couple of gigs in New York City; he told me he was nervous because he hadn't played the banjo live for a paying audience in over thirty years. He continued writing new tunes and began thinking of doing a CD. Between the material that first appeared on *The Steve Martin Brothers* and his fresh crop of five-string fillies, he soon had an album's worth of material.

A studio was secured in New Jersey, a band selected and with John McEuen in the production chair and suggestions floating in from the peanut gallery, recording began in June of 2008.

The album has met with much deserved critical acclaim and the accompanying tablature is in your hands. Steve and I spent a good number of hours playing through all this music to make sure it was accurate. It's been a pleasure and an honor to work with Steve. His generosity of spirit pervades everything he does. I can feel it in this music, and I hope you can too. *

Tony Trischka
April 2009

*I don't know Tony Trischka. I don't know why he's written this book about me. It's weird.
—*Steve Martin*

NOTES ON THE TUNINGS
By Steve Martin

As a reader of tabs and not of music, I can get very confused by alternate tunings. So here's my quick and dirty explanation of the various ones I use:

Open G: Nothing more to be said here.

Open D: I use this for "Freddie's Lilt," "Words Unspoken," "Clawhammer Medley," and "Hoedown at Alice's." If you use D tuners, this is what they down-tune to. Almost. To put your banjo in open D, tune your third string down to match the fourth string at the fourth fret, then tune your second string to match your third string at the third fret. Then tune your fifth string up to match your first string at the seventh fret (or use a fifth string capo). Easy!

G Modal: I use this tuning for "Saga of the Old West." Starting in open G, simply tune your second string up a half step so it matches the third string at the fifth fret.

C Modal (or **Double C**): I use this tuning for "The Crow." Start in G modal tuning, then lower the fourth string one full note, so when the fourth is fretted at the seventh fret, it matches the third string.

D tuning: I use this tuning for "Tin Roof," and "Blue River Waltz." Starting in open G, raise the fifth string one full note, so it matches the first string at the 7th fret.

DADDY PLAYED THE BANJO

By Steve Martin and Gary Scruggs

Not much to say about this tune; the words are everything. The banjo is there to give the lyrics a context. Clawhammer style (will I ever get used to that word? I always called it frailing) brings a lonesome atmosphere and vivid picture to the song.

—*Steve Martin*

Key of A, Capo 2
Tuning: g D G B D (Open G Tuning), Clawhammer

Verse

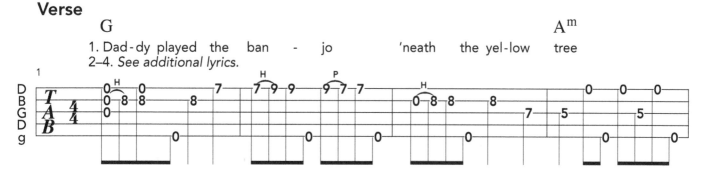

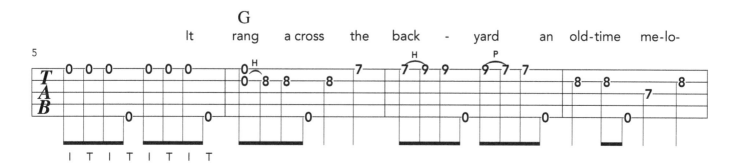

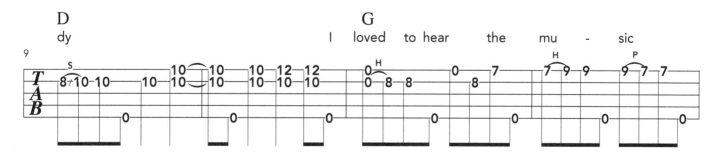

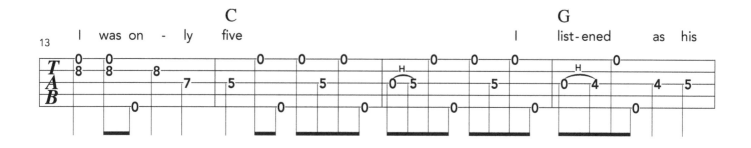

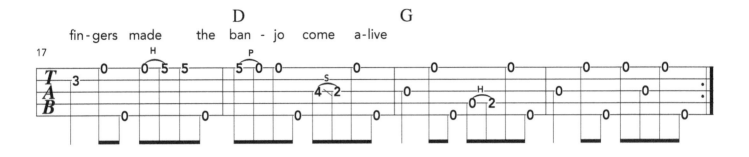

Bridge

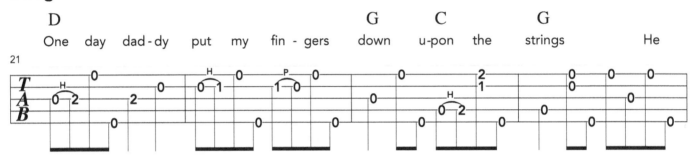

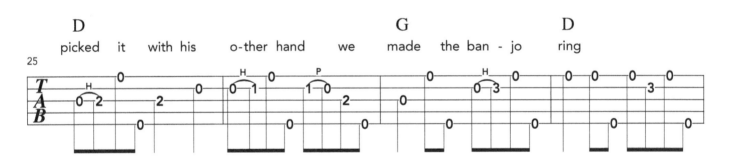

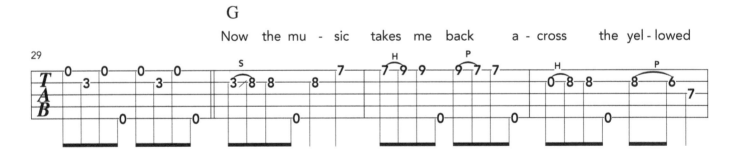

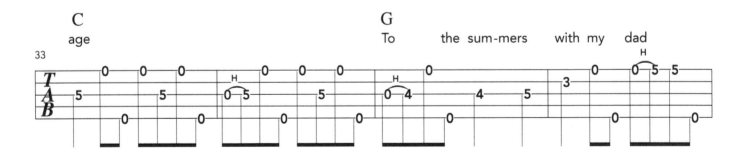

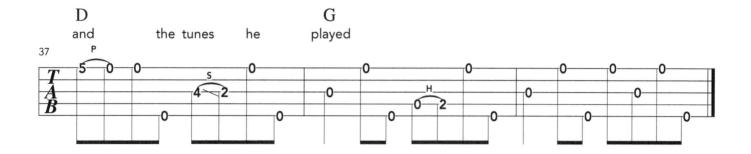

1. Daddy played the banjo 'neath the yellow tree
    It rang across the backyard, an old-time melody
    I loved to hear the music, I was only five
    I listened as his fingers made the banjo come alive

2. Sometimes I'd wake up at night and hear a distant tune
    The banjo would echo around my childhood room
    I'd sneak down the back stairs, daddy never knew
    I'd grab a broom and make believe I was pickin' too

    Bridge
    One day daddy put my fingers down upon the strings
    He picked with his other hand, we made the banjo ring
    Now the music takes me back across the yellowed age
    To the summers with my dad and the tunes he played

3. But I'm just telling lies about the things I did
    See, I'm that banjo player who never had a kid
    Now I sit beneath that yellow tree
    Hoping that a kid somewhere is listening to me

4. Daddy played the banjo 'neath the yellow tree
    It rang across the backyard and wove a spell on me
    Now the banjo takes me back through the foggy haze
    Where memories of what never was become the good old days

PITKIN COUNTY TURNAROUND

This song is bluegrass and it should be played accordingly. On the record, John McEuen plays a double banjo section to back me up, but the double banjo effect is not necessary to the song.

—Steve Martin

Tuning: g D G B D (Open G Tuning)

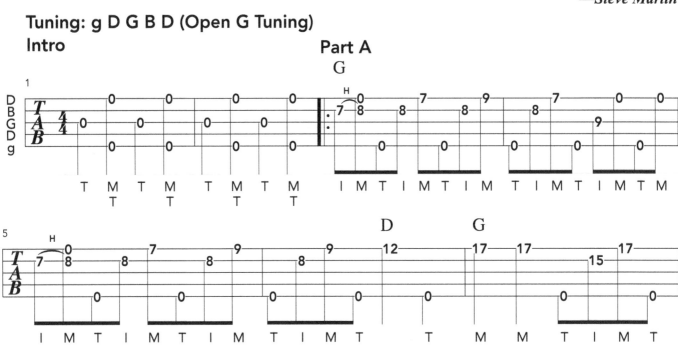

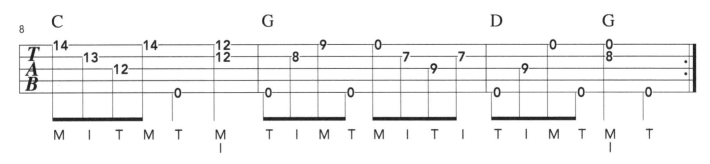

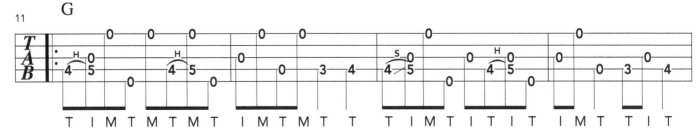

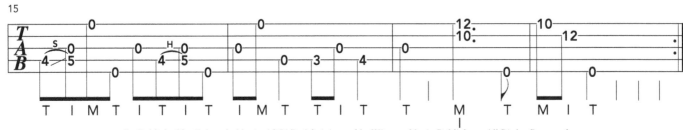

HOEDOWN AT ALICE'S

In the B section, the first several notes are produced by a hammer-on at the fourth and third strings, at the fourth and third frets respectively. Even though the notes are picked, it's important to hammer-on *hard*. This produces some extra, in-between, reverberant notes.

—*Steve Martin*

Tuning: a D F♯ A D (Open D Tuning)

Part A

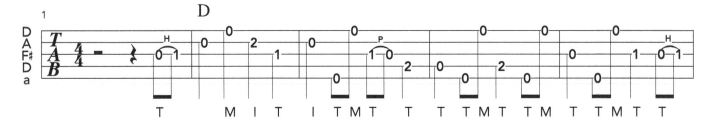

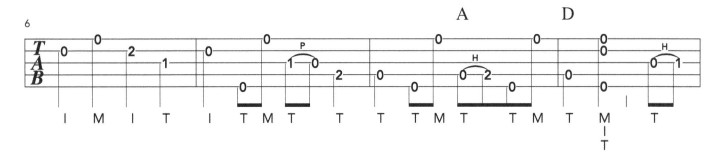

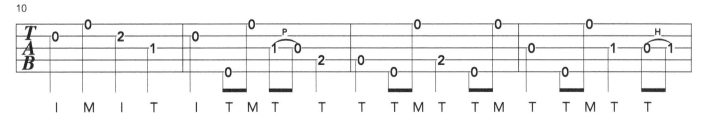

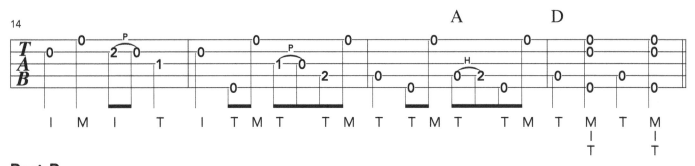

Part B

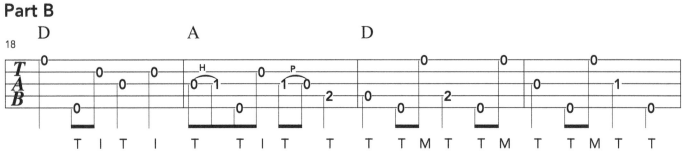

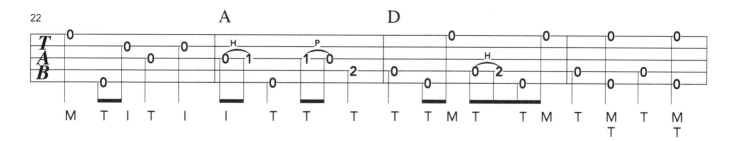

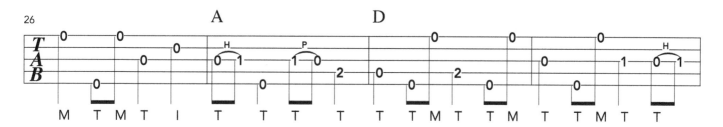

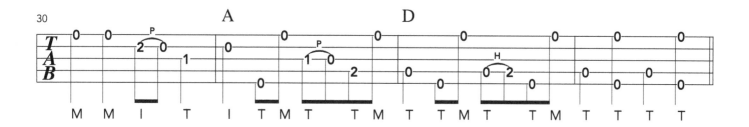

Part C

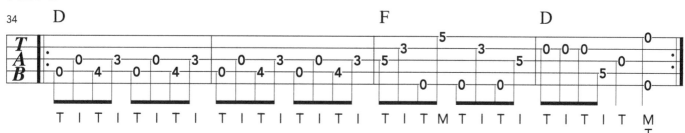

Part D

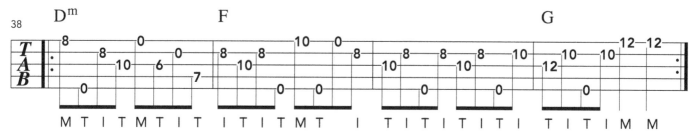

Part E

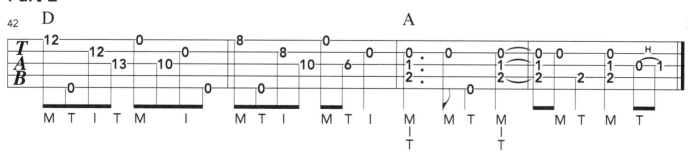

LATE FOR SCHOOL

I wrote this first as an instrumental, and love to hear it played that way. My ideal in the song is to subtly retard the pull-offs as the song progresses, until it feels like the subsequent phrases have to "catch up" to the rhythm. To do the pull-off on the fourth string at the third fret, I lift my third finger off the C chord and reach over to the fourth string.

—Steve Martin

Tuning: g D G B D (Open G Tuning), Clawhammer

Part A (Verse)

Alternate Measures 4, 5, and 6 (Part A)

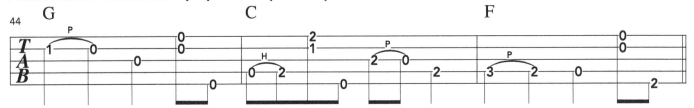

1. Woke up this morning, clock said I was late for school
   Teacher told me "that's not cool," gotta put my shirt and pants on
   Flew down the front stair, wet my fingers and slicked my hair
   Elbowed grandma passing by, her face went into a pie
   If I'm late there's misery, I won't be up on history
   I'll be in the English grammar slammer and I'll get a C
   Got a warning last semester, told my mom and that depressed her
   Promised dad I won't be late, so gotta accelerate

2. Ran out the front door, moving like a meteor
   I sped across the front lawn quickly, missed the bus, my shoelace tripped me
   Rounded the corner, homework flying as I go
   Neighbor shouted "tally ho!" and gave a standing O
   Leapt across three lawn flamingos, waved to Sal, he's Filipino
   Jumped a fence and found that I was headed toward a pool
   In the air, I did look funny, on T.V. I'd make some money
   Waved my arms and legs like mad to alter where I'd land

3. Aimed for the rubber boat, hit instead the kiddie float
   I began to lose control, I'm so glad I learned to log roll
   Jumped onto the diving board, bounced off it and headed toward
   A jungle gym, I swung just right and caught onto a kite (Whoa! I'm flying!)

4. Up so high I see the school, 8 a.m., that's the rule
   Flying slowly, time is marking, down below the dogs are barking
   I feel like I'm sailing, but—uh oh—the wind is failing!
   Now I'm headed downward, groundward, clown-ward to the school
   On the football field I crash, 50 yard line—perfect smash
   Grab my books and so begins my frantic final dash
   Down the hall I ricochet, trophy cases in the way
   The other kids are all in class, I wish that I were they!

5. I see the clock hands with delight, 8 a.m., exactly right
   Pull the handle with a fight, door is locked and that's not right
   There's not a person here today, is everybody out to play?
   Now I'm thinking—and it's sinking in—it's Saturday! (Aw, rats! I could have stayed in bed)

6. I'm out the school gate, wish that I could aviate
   Or possibly evaporate, I'll be home and back in bed soon
   My dad is waiting, "what the heck were you up to?
   Let's go fishing, my oh my, your grandma's face was in a pie"
   This is really something, I'm with dad and fish are jumping
   Mom gave me a new alarm to set for Monday morn
   Never want to be late for school, never want to be the classroom fool
   I'd be in the English grammar slammer and I'd get a D
   Now my feet are doing dances, hip hooray for second chances
   I'm not late and life is great, it's time to celebrate, whoo!

TIN ROOF

This tune is played in D tuning (as opposed to Open D), which is simply G tuning with the fifth string tuned up to A. I find the song works best when not played too fast, and the emphasis in the first section is on making it sound Oh So Sweet. The second section does require some quick up and down the neck chord changes, and the third section, which I refer to as the "raindrops" section, is all about sensitivity and feel. In the part where two strings are played simultaneously, I find it's easier if I mentally seal my first and second finger together. Occasionally, during this part, I tap the head with my little finger, adding a faint, percussive effect.

—Steve Martin

Tuning: a D G B D (D Tuning)

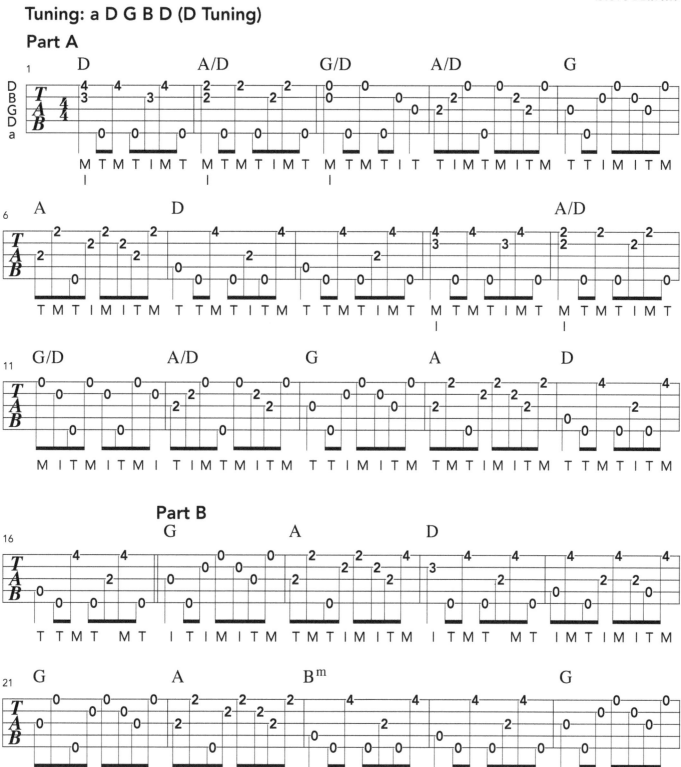

15

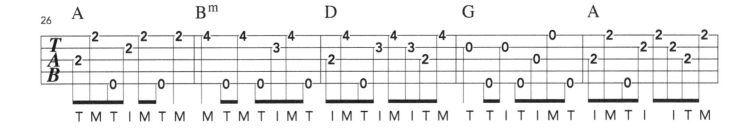

Part C

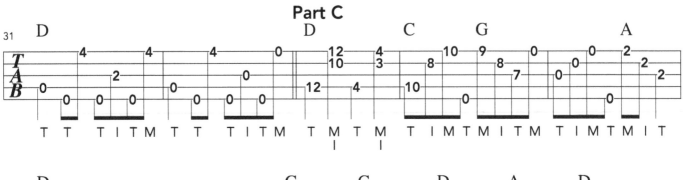

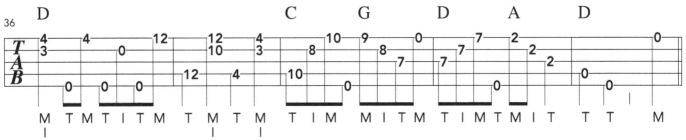

Part D

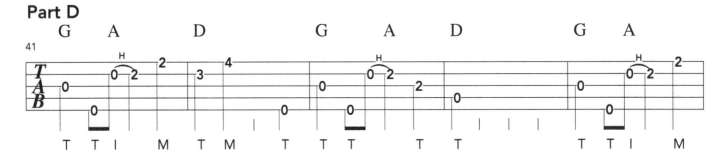

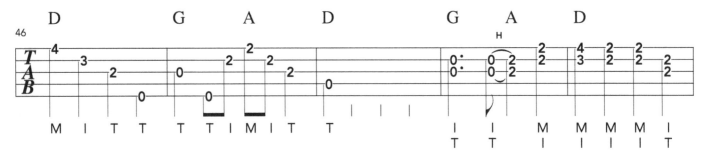

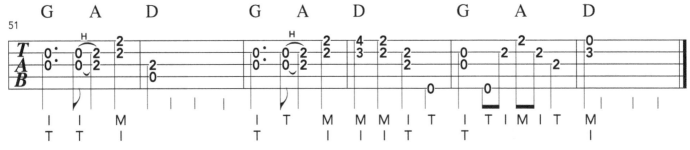

WORDS UNSPOKEN

By Steve Martin and Pete Wernick

This song is completely about feel. Let your emotions wander and play each melody note as though it were a word (incidentally, there are words to this song, written by Pete Wernick and myself, but that will be for later exposure).

Pete played the "B" section of the song, and recorded it with his banjo tuned to open G, while I played the "A" section in open D. This makes an accurate tab impossible, unless you can retune your banjo in a gnat's breath. For completeness, I figured out a simple approximation of Pete's section for open D tuning, but it's nice to hear the song with two banjos in different tunings.

It should be noted that in measures three and five, there is a pull-off that is delayed by one note, occurring on the first string, pulling off from the second fret to open.

—*Steve Martin*

Tuning: a D F♯ A D (Open D Tuning)

Part A

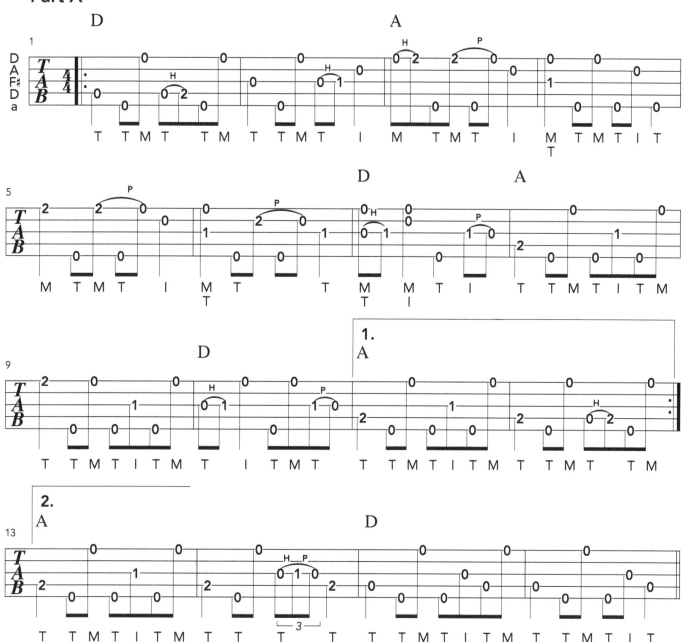

Part B

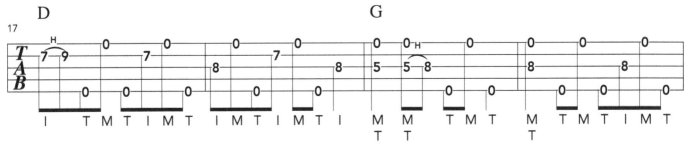

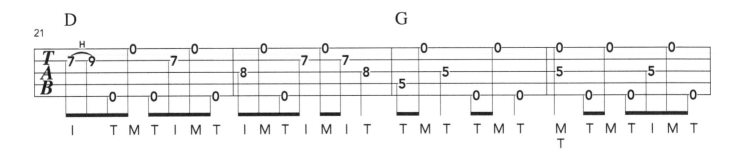

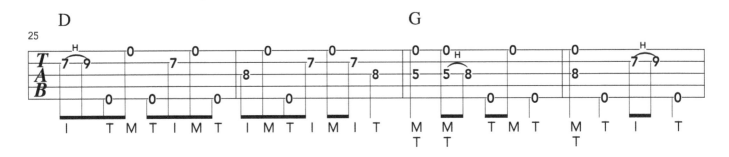

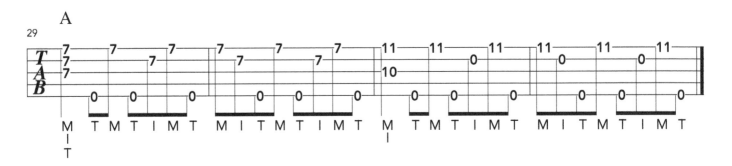

Alternate Last Two Measures   ## Alternate Last Two Measures (Part 2)

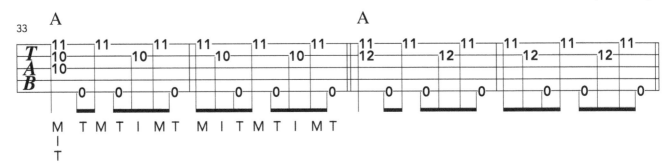

PRETTY FLOWERS

Again, the banjo is strictly backup, played with an old-fashioned simplicity, but appropriate for this little tune. A slight oddity happens between measures two and three (and between measures six and seven, and fourteen and fifteen): one note is picked but two notes are hammered on, which delivers a distant echo. For our recording, we tuned the banjo down to E to accommodate Dolly and Vince's vocal range, but the song is easily sung in G, especially by a castrato.

—*Steve Martin*

1. If I gave you pretty flowers
   If I took you out to dinner
   If we walked home by the river
   Would you invite me in?

2. If we sat down on the sofa
   If I told you funny stories
   If I moved a little closer
   Would you put your hand in mine?

   Chorus
   If I told you you were lovely
   If I put my arm around you
   If I touched you on the shoulder
   Would you rest your hand on mine?

3. If I took you out to dinner
   If I moved a little closer
   And I touched you on the shoulder
   Would you make love to me?

Chorus
Oh my darling, I have loved you
Since you took me out to dinner
Since we walked down by the river
Over 30 years ago

Chorus
When you told me that you loved me
I hadn't felt so lovely
Since the day I decided
That I would marry you

4. Well I took you out to dinner
   And I told you funny stories
   And I moved a little closer
   And you made love to me

5. If I gave you pretty flowers
   If I took you out to dinner
   If we walked down by the river
   La, la, la, la, la, la, la

WALLY ON THE RUN

For the opening passages, simply plant your middle finger on the second string at the eighth fret and just leave it there. There's something nice about watching the remaining fingers dance around the imaginary X that the other fretted strings make. This song, like Pitkin, is bluegrass, so *drive* is everything.

—*Steve Martin*

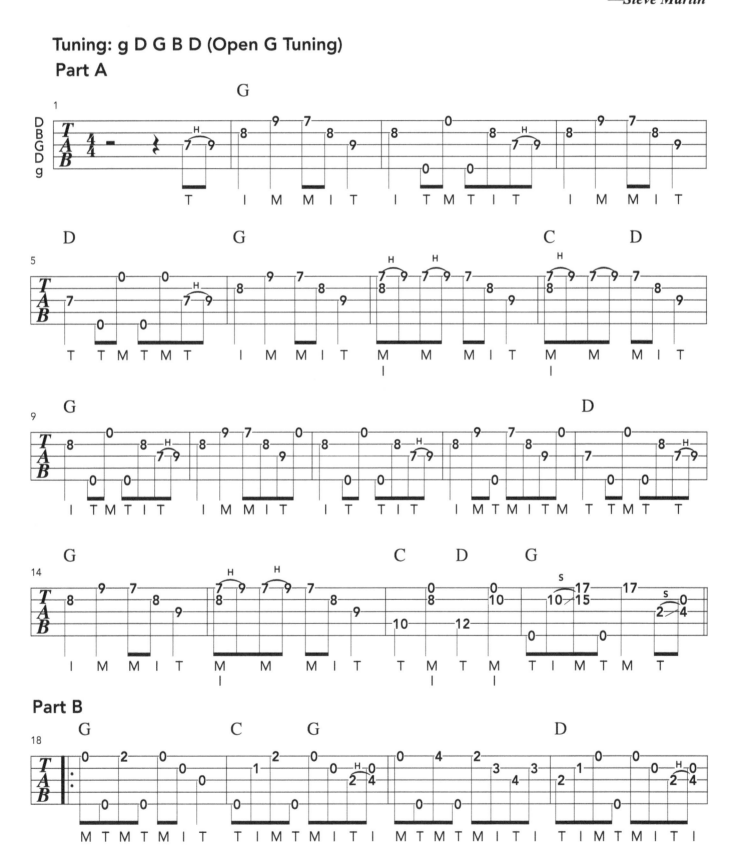

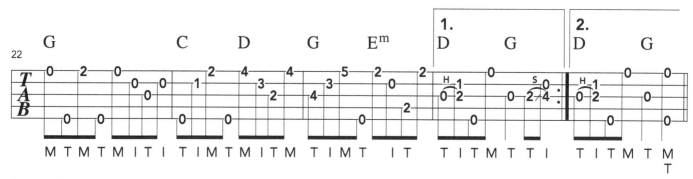

Part C

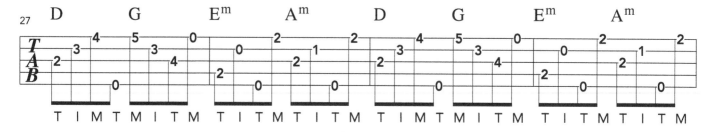

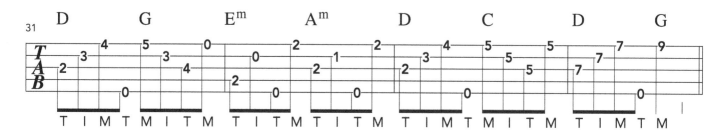

Harmony

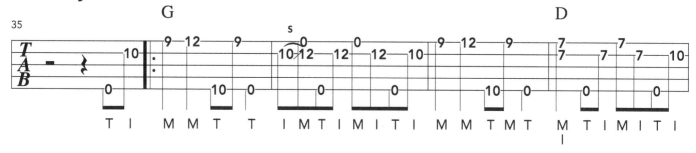

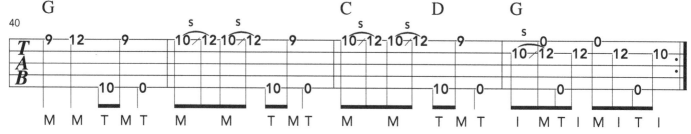

Ending

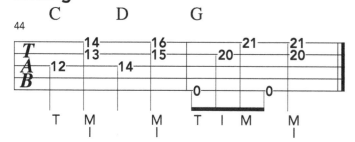

FREDDIE'S LILT

Played in open D tuning, this song utilizes the overtones of unplucked strings. I recommend fretting the full chords down the neck (but not up the neck), even though all the strings are not plucked. In the fourth measure, depress the fourth string at the second fret, and the third string at the first fret. These strings, even though they are not sounded, create a harmonic resonance, whatever that means.

—*Steve Martin*

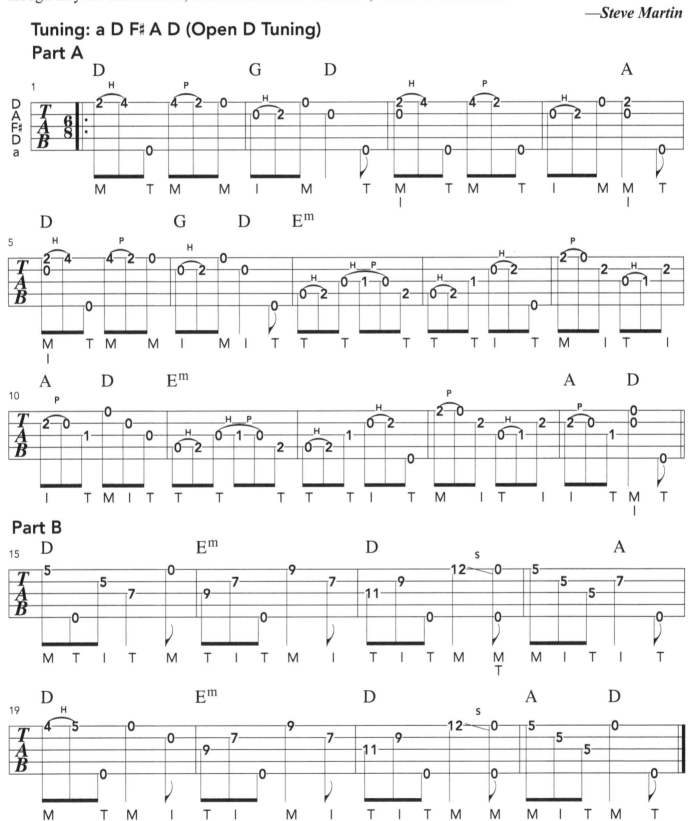

SAGA OF THE OLD WEST

If you like to hammer on and pull off, you'll be in heaven. Also, the initial melody can, with the exception of one note, be played entirely with the thumb only, and that is the way I often play it. The second time around, I like to play the melody with all three fingers as it allows an extra punch in the attack. In this song, when a brush (B) is indicated, it is done with the thumb but limited to the fourth and third strings.

—*Steve Martin*

Tuning: g D G C D (G Modal Tuning)

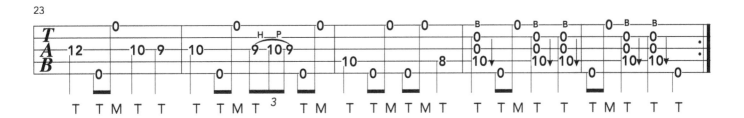

Part D

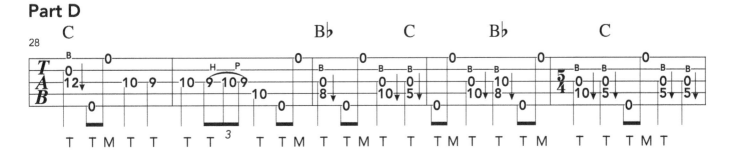

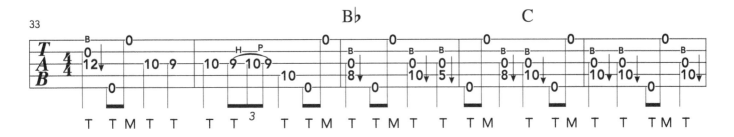

Part E

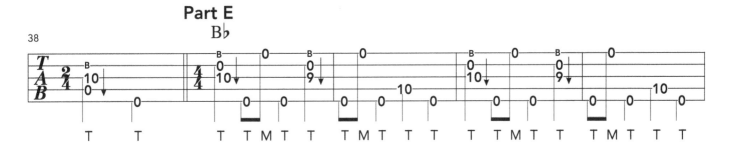

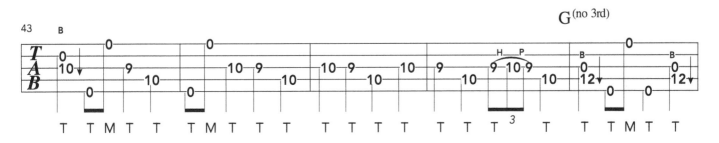

Ending

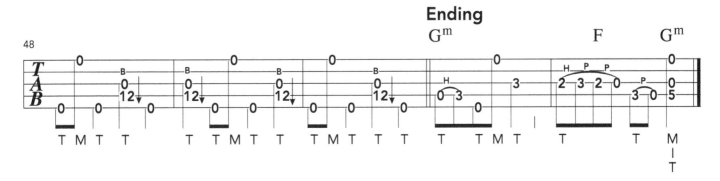

CLAWHAMMER MEDLEY

Traditional, Arranged by Steve Martin

I play the entire melodies of these songs almost exclusively on the first string, allowing the banjo to resonate with nice, airy overtones. I like to make full chords down the neck, even though all the strings are not struck, as the chord is lightly sounded as a hammer-on.

In the closing section of "Simple Gifts," a brush is indicated, which I learned from the old Pete Seeger book, "How to Play the Five String Banjo." The way I do it, the hand unrolls, little finger first, stopping with the middle finger. The thumb stays connected to the first finger to hold my place over the banjo.

—Steve Martin

Tuning: a D F♯ A D (Open D Tuning)

"Sally Ann"

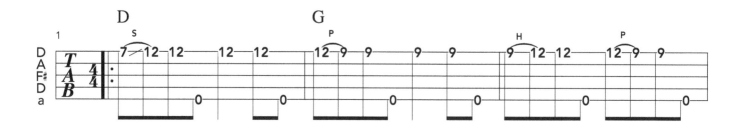

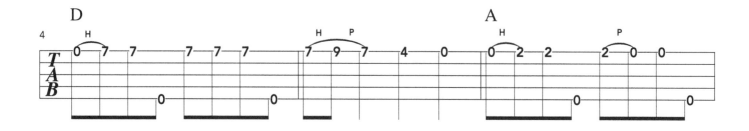

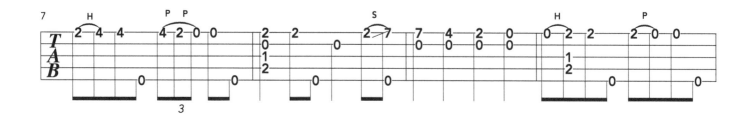

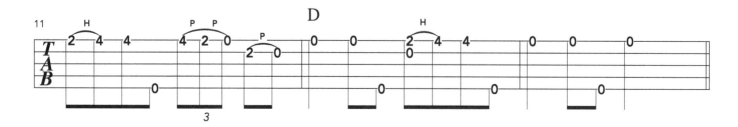

"The Johnson Boys"

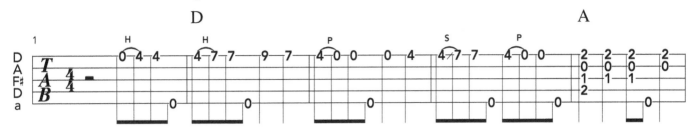

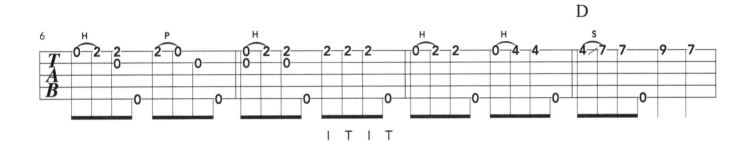

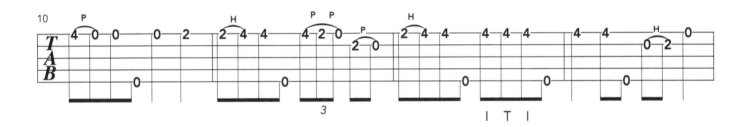

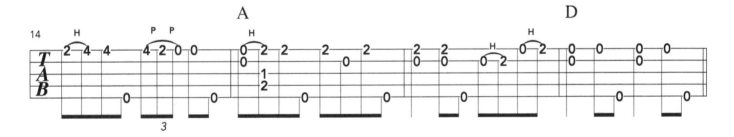

"Simple Gifts"

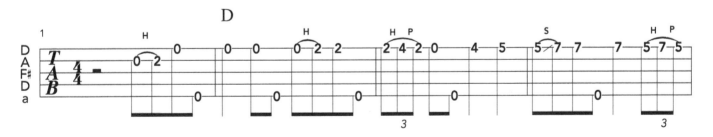

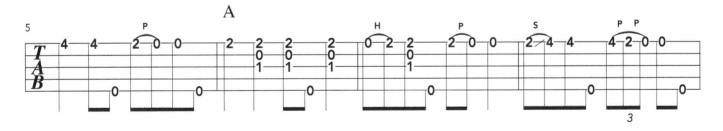

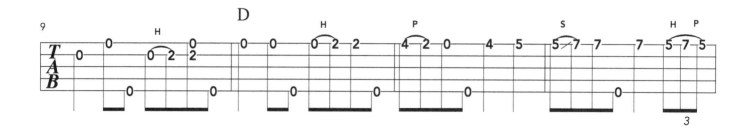

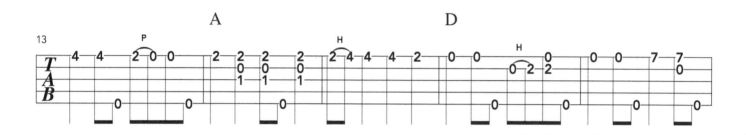

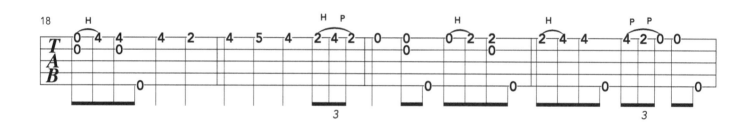

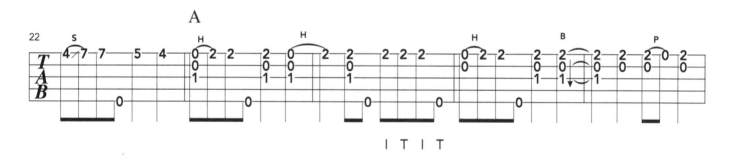

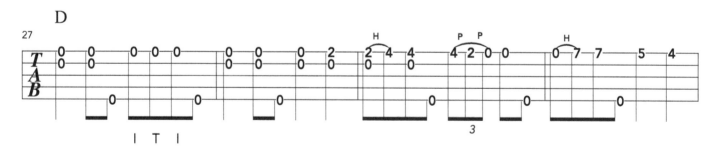

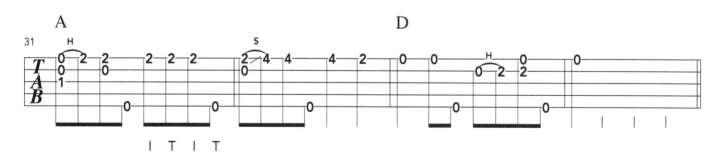

"Loch Lomond"

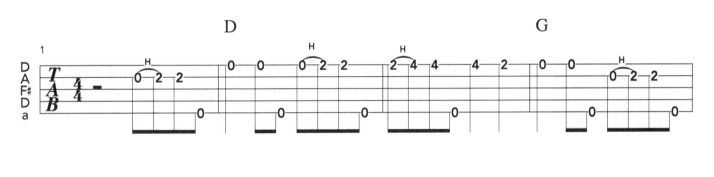

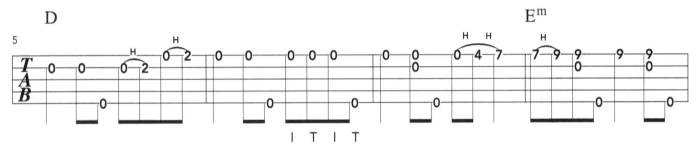

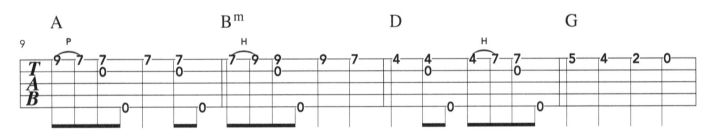

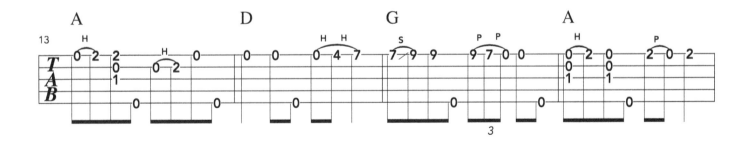

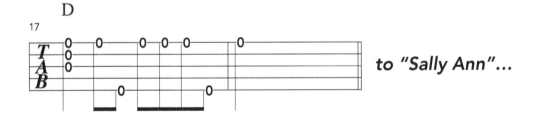

to "Sally Ann"...

CALICO TRAIN

When I play this song, my main goal is perfectly timed notes, or as my friend John McEuen called them, "bullets." Also, in the first section, it might help to imagine that the melody, first played with the thumb, is being "handed off" to the first finger, then "handed back" to the thumb.

I found over the years that I started to occasionally bring my first finger over to the fourth string when the thumb would normally be used, a technique which is involved in this song, and a few others in this book. I'm not sure what difference it makes; at first it was convenience, but I think it delivers a rhythmic kick and extra volume.

In part D, the brush is done with the back of the fourth finger.

—*Steve Martin*

Key of B♭, Capo 3
Tuning: g D G B D (Open G Tuning)

Part A (Verse)

1. When you said good - bye
2–4. See additional lyrics.

thought I would cry Or at least feel the

dark of a deep shade of blue I would

have to at - tend to a heart on the

30

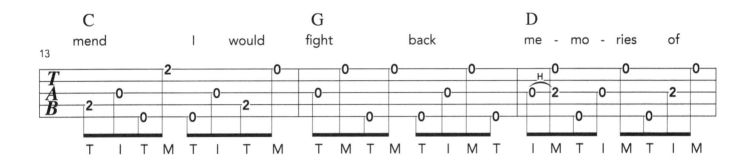

Part B (Chorus)

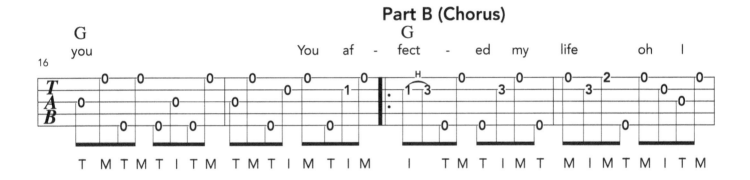

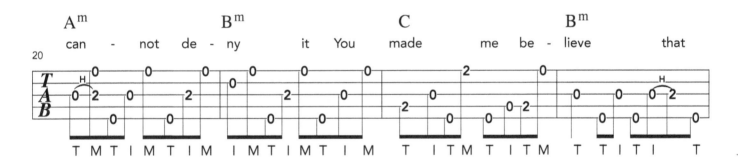

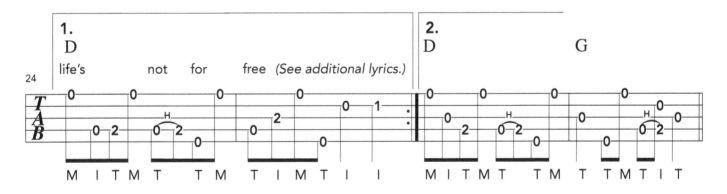

Part C

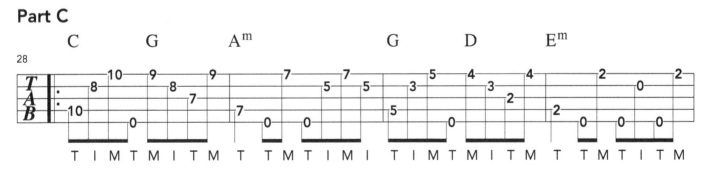

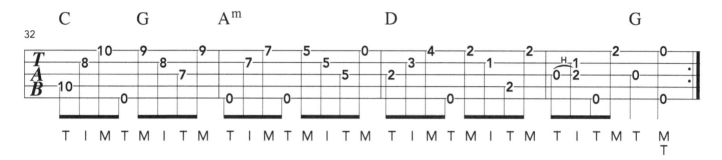

Part D

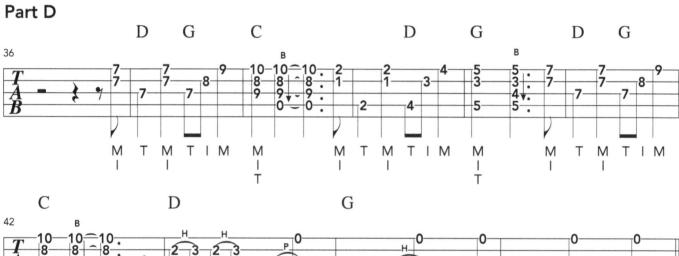

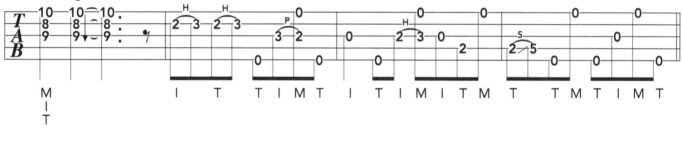

Part A (First Variation), then Part B

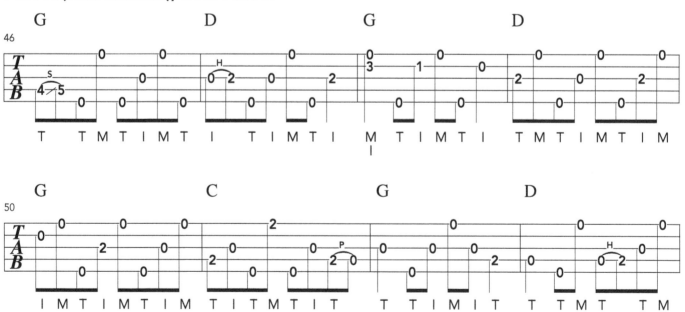

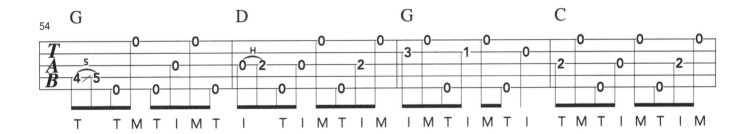

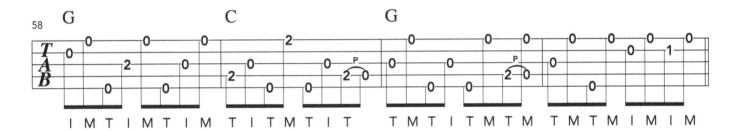

Part A (First Four Measures of Second Variation)

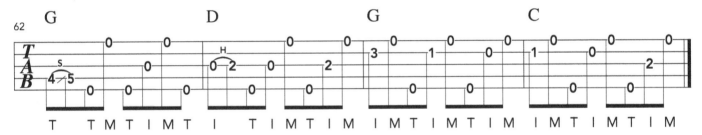

1. When you said goodbye, I thought I would cry
   Or at least feel the dark of a deep shade of blue
   I would have to attend to a heart on the mend
   I would fight back my memories of you

   Chorus
   You affected my life, oh I cannot deny it
   You made me believe that life's not for free
   But anger and scorn are not what I'm built for
   So, my darling, I leave that to you

2. I sat one night in the glow of firelight
   And I played all my favorite tunes you disliked
   Some friends made a call, let's go casual
   Tonight is the Calico Ball

   Chorus
   Now I'm feeling alive with a man on each side
   With my heart leaning toward the most apropos
   And each swing round the room lifts and spins off the gloom:
   And every step takes me further from you

3. That night at the dance after our long romance
   Made me feel like a woman in bloom
   Romance it is true, it is useful for youth
   But for me now my star is the truth

   Chorus
   Then a man came to me, I said "yes, I am free"
   And I undid the clasp of my gold ball and chain
   I danced in his charms, was completely disarmed
   Now I'm riding along on the Calico Train

4. Sorrow and strain, they can both long remain
   They can take you and leave you alone and in pain
   But freedom's in sight, if the road in the night
   Is lit by the light of the Calico Train

   Chorus
   Joy is the word now that's guiding my life
   My step is much quicker since you said goodbye
   The blood flowing through me has turned to champagne
   Now I'm riding along on the Calico Train

BANANA BANJO

This is ostensibly the most difficult song on the album, but really it's just chord positions bouncing up and down the neck. In fact, there's hardly a moment when one chord is more than two frets from the last. The rhythm of the middle section might be difficult to understand through tablature, so I advise getting the chord structure from the book, and the syncopation from listening to the record over and over and over and over (and over).

—*Steve Martin*

Tuning: g D G B D (Open G Tuning)
Part A

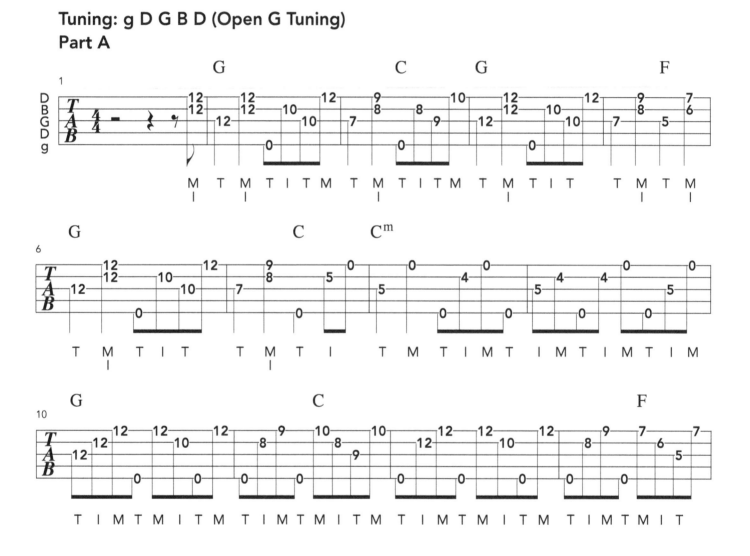

Part B'

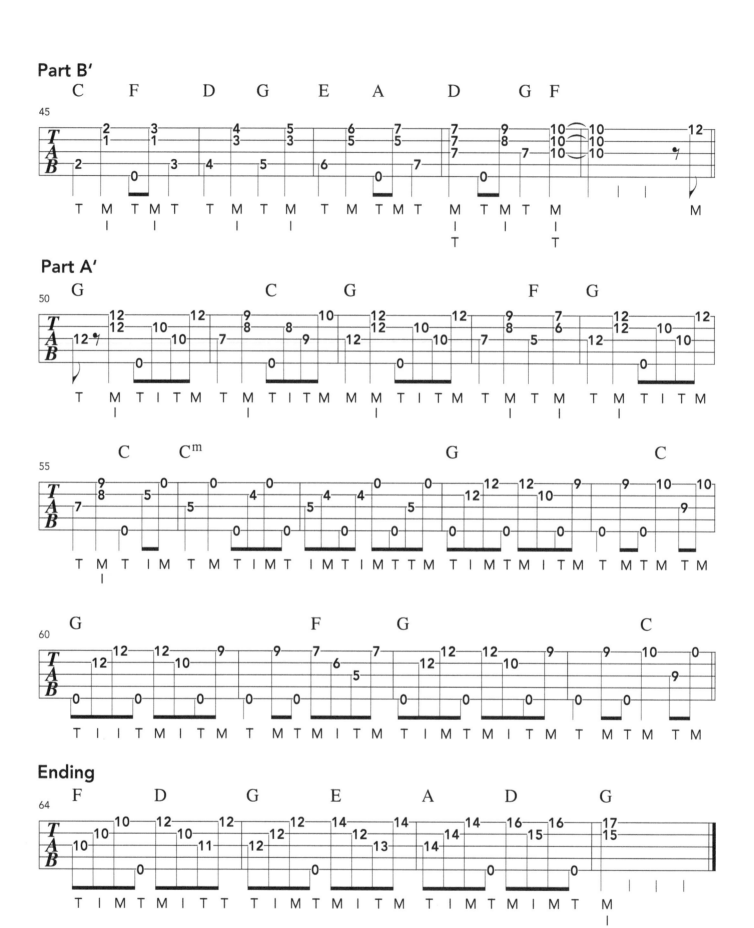

Part A'

Ending

BLUE RIVER WALTZ

This is a relatively straight-forward waltz. The second section, what I think of as the "Irish" section, is best when the fill behind the melody is so casually expressed that it can barely be heard.

—Steve Martin

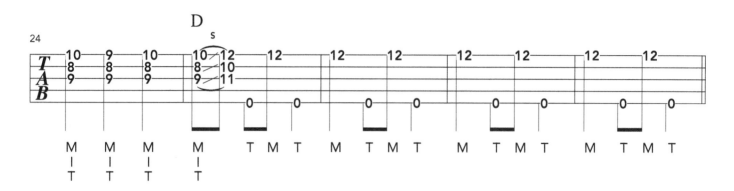

Part D

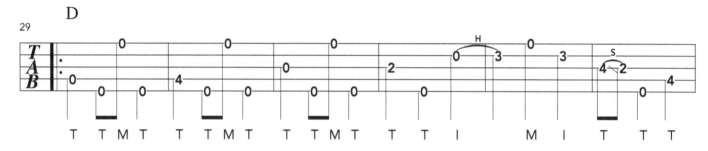

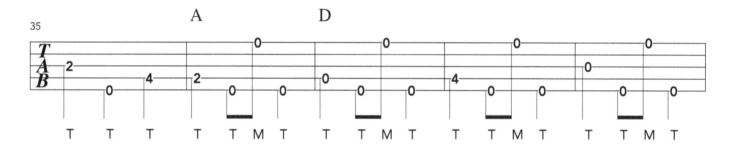

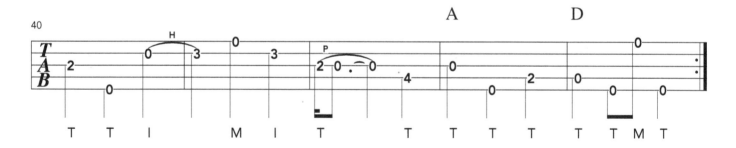

THE CROW

It's embarrassing how little movement the left hand makes in playing the main theme. When I play this on stage, I almost feel motionless, especially when Tony Trischka is with me playing the up-the-neck break with his hand flying all over the fingerboard. Too bad I don't have a "How Strong Are You" circus mallet to whack him over the head.

 The crucial elements in the song are drama and a slight hint of syncopation. On the record, Tony provides a sensational double banjo section, and contributes a superior – and difficult – middle break (the final section of the break was devised by Béla Fleck), but the song can be played without them. Tony's (and Béla's) sensational breaks are not tabbed here because they would probably demand something like money.

—*Steve Martin*

Melody

Tuning: g D G C D (C Modal Tuning)
Part A

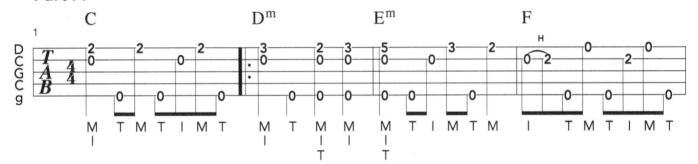

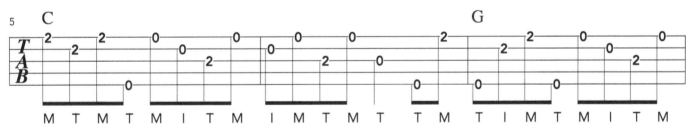

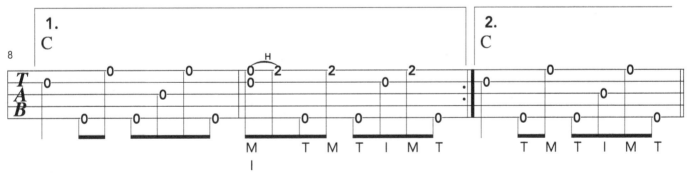

Part B

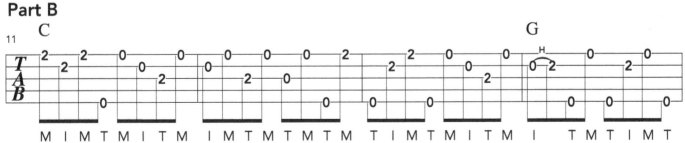

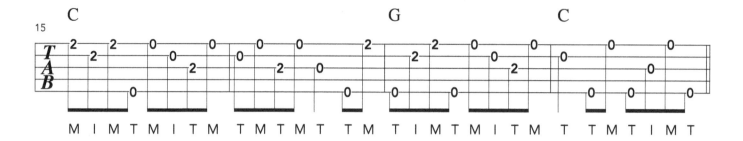

Part C

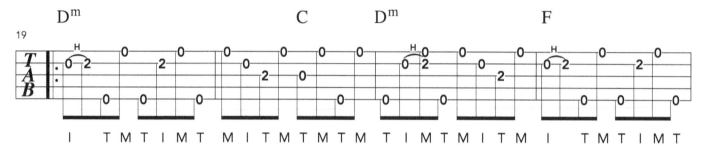

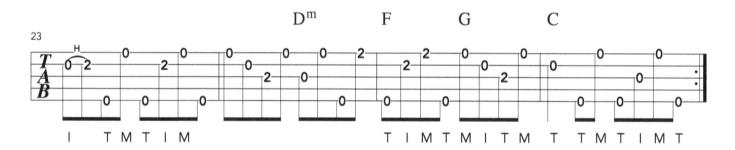

Harmony

Tuning: g D G B D (Open G Tuning)

Part A

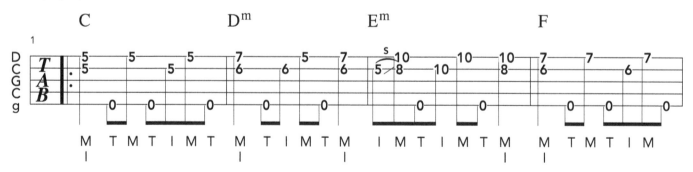

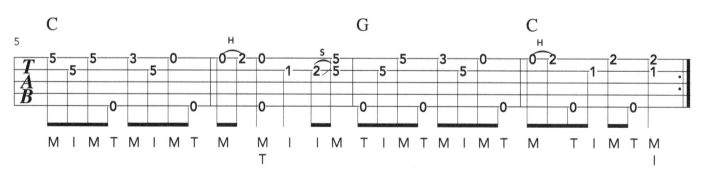

Part B

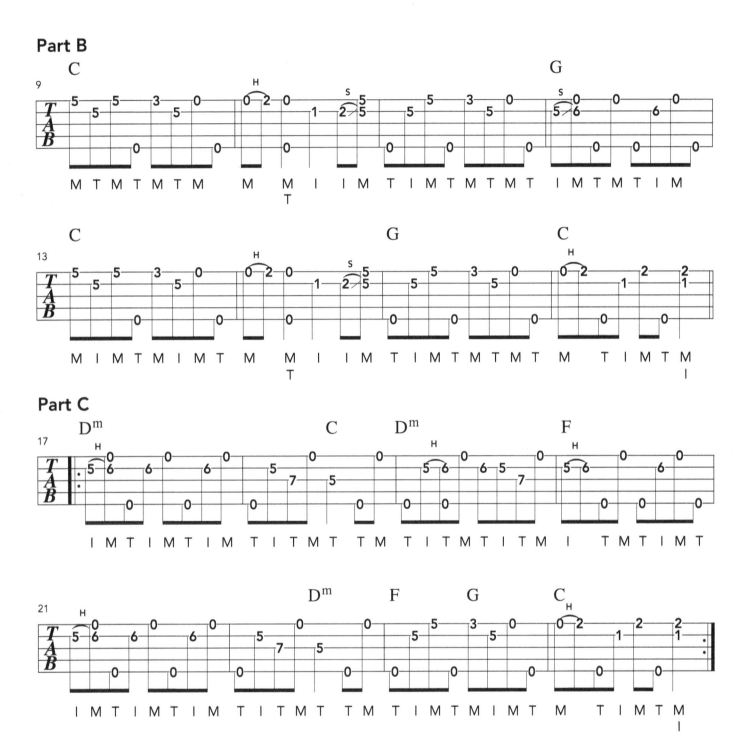

Part C

Transcription: Tony Trischka

Music Engraving and Layout: Andrew DuBrock